I0210976

In the Wake

poems by

Ariel Machell

Finishing Line Press
Georgetown, Kentucky

In the Wake

ACKNOWLEDGMENTS

"Questions Without Resolution in the Wake of Bearable Loss" was published
in longer form in *The Inflectionist Review*. Gratitude to John Sibley Williams,
whose keen editorial eye opened the floodgates, and marked the beginning
of the inspiration to begin this manuscript.

With thanks also to *Laurel Review* for naming *In the Wake* a finalist in the
2023 Midwest Chapbook Contest.

And thanks to *Black Lawrence Press* for naming *In the Wake* a semifinalist
for the Spring 2023 Black River Chapbook Competition.

And to my friends, without whom there would be no reason to write.

An excerpt of *In the Wake* was published in *Laurel Review* Issue 57.1 as part
of the finalist series.

Publisher: Leah Huete de Maines
Editor: Christen Kincaid
Cover Art: Virginia Deaver
Author Photo: Ariel Machell
Cover Design: Elizabeth Maines McCleavy

Order online: www.finishinglinepress.com
also available on amazon.com

Author inquiries and mail orders:
Finishing Line Press
PO Box 1626
Georgetown, Kentucky 40324
USA

For M, C, D, L, & L
With thanks to the Willamette River

"We talked about it late last night and in the voice
of my friend, there was a thin wire of grief, a tone
almost querulous. After a while I understood that,
talking this way, everything dissolves…"

"These are the dog days,
unvaried
except by accident,
mist rising from soaked lawns,
gone world…"

—Robert Hass

Before Memory was born, Memory slept in a dark, wet place, but it was warm, like an indoor pool after hours, and Memory floated easily, though Memory didn't yet know how to swim, how to tread water for leisure or for life. While drifting, Memory'd often hear a voice, but Memory's ears were stoppered, and nebulous. They sloshed with a blue pain, and the voice was only a thrum, only a gurgle, only a far-off song. Meaning and shape were lost to Memory, but there was pulse, and there was cadence, and there was flow, so Memory learned to hum before Memory learned to swim.

What governs the world?

Imperfectible afternoon. Not unkind summer.
Shadow of water. Musk of dog.

When did the heart become an affliction?

Scuffling down the same trail each morning, D and I, a long walk that left us nowhere, mouths coffee-dry and pursed with thoughts unspoken. How many gifts. How much time. What bird is that. Long fingers. *Brief* is a good thing. To hold something briefly is to open it to a cherishing. These were my thoughts. I can't say what his were. The dream he had, dissolving. Only the middle distance remained. What was left behind. What was staring us in the face. Drought. Doubt. My hopeless sense of direction. The compass said true North, but it wasn't right. I said nothing. It wasn't right.

Am I cowardly? A friend who was once a lover asked *What do you believe?* I said only *The universe is vast.* Those days, I let Possibility do all the heavy work. I couldn't commit to anything, and Possibility committed to everything. The truth is, I believed only in rivers. The truth is, I almost died on one. In one. No, beneath one. The truth is, I saw nothing. I saw absence. A wash. Arroyo. Gully. Gulch. When I came up, the river was gleaming, and sharp, like a kindness. And blue, as I remembered it. Blue, as I have never seen it.

Morning's light like a lesson today,

the clear sky condescending down.
Even with eyes shut it invades—

pure, wretched hue drenching everything it touches.

Memory sleeps in the basement with a sleeping bag and a flashlight and a brand new pack of Nutter Butters, tornado sirens blaring, the power still working, five of Memory's favorite VHS tapes dragged down the stairs. Memory sits criss-cross-apple-sauce and repeats words from the first film. *Bottomless. Fathoms. Reprimand. Shore. Daughter.* The VCR's a little finicky and the screen a little fuzzy, but actually, Memory is happy and not at all scared, like the time Memory fell off the boat without a life preserver, the way the warm water wrapped around Memory like a promise and filled Memory's open eyes like a blindfold and entered Memory's mouth like a lullaby. Memory wants to stay in this perfect dark like the bottom of a lake, here, beneath the house where Memory can't see out the windows, where Memory can't see the rain fall or the wind blow, can't see the blue sky turn red with rise and set. Memory likes having a reason to hide.

Will my new silver watch break on a Monday or a Friday? There are no trivial questions. Days I held inside me as potential occurrences. There are no inconsequentials. I only started keeping time after meeting D. To gift a watch is to promise. What does the passage of time promise but a collection of things? There is nothing I will not collect.

A cursory google search tells me the word *scourge* can be used for a group of mosquitoes. I can't remember if I looked that up this morning or five years ago. Nothing is linear but the mosquito's beak. Walking up. Waking up. Five years ago, I woke and walked barefoot on a bed of moss with M and joked about wanting it as a rug in our living room. Might we have just moved out? Stayed there in that green place forever? Now, touching moss only feels like loss. Writing that, I asked myself, *Is that cheesy?* It's at least true.

M in the water with me, C feeding his fire, L and L and D standing round. My thighs got the brunt of it, and my ass, swimming that July, slipping silkily on algae-slicked rocks, the swarm that followed me, the scourge that loved me so incompletely, talking, taking. Kisses that swelled from the sweetness, then bruised, leaving marks that time stored away. Our smiles, like the pools, dried up. Secrets swallowed. Silk handkerchief torn. All the severed threads.

While we slept fitfully, vespertilian night winged in, feeding on overripe fruit from the kitchen, the marionberries we picked, the single, pocket-carried quince spewing its aromas.

Little evidence left behind, but for the empty spaces.

From which animal did this hair come?

Hangover. Consume. Over-
hang. The cons of assuming.

What were we willing to ignore?

Memory sleeps in the attic like a box of Christmas ornaments. Like a box of camping supplies. Like a box of family memorabilia. Like a box of important documents. Memory wonders how important Memory is, sleeping in the attic as Memory does. Memory can't leave because Memory won't leave. Memory sings all day and sleeps all day and recounts the days. Memory says words like invocations—*Inlet. In. Let. Fleet. Flee. Feet. Runnel. Run. Null.*— splitting them open like loon eggs on the attic's shore, finding the cracks in the creeks, distributaries distributed into the air. In the attic, seasons impose like bad thoughts and pollute the air. Memory takes notes and stuffs them in the walls for insulation. Every so often, Nostalgia visits and brings photos of beautiful people, and candles with beautiful smells, but Nostalgia won't tell Memory who they're of, what they're imitating, all the parts that make them. Nostalgia's visits are too brief. Memory wants to know when Nostalgia's coming back.

How to breathe without thinking *Am I breathing?*

The idea of lungs, no, the image
of lungs, no, the feel of lungs, no,

the faith of lungs, no—

I talk about my time there. A new friend asks *Did you ever drink from the river?*

Did we drink from the river? No, but we're still full on the river. We're greedy for the river. We're sick of the river. Singing inside us.

The river is not blue. It is only the reflection of the sky, also not blue. Let's argue. At what point does perception become reality? If the river had a soul, it would still not be blue. Now you say, *but the river does have a soul*, and I say, *but is it blue?* And you say, *it is nothing, not blue, not any color.* And I say, *how can you possess nothing?* And you say, *we all do.*

Departure is what makes possible return. The not-blue surface twinkles in the rearview. We eat ice cream from Prince Puckler's and soothe our sunburned shoulders barely. *The only emperor is the emperor of ice-cream*, we say to each other, running tongues along the melting dribbles, imperfectly rounded scoops dissolving. We eat. Until it's all gone, we eat.

The line in italics refers to the Wallace Stevens poem of the same name.

Despite the days we floated endlessly, we spent most of our mornings and nights thinking about what made an ending. *How* to end, *where* to end. Beginnings were easy. But endings? I'd always miss the finish line, walk right past it, go for miles more, confessions spilling from my lips with every step. And now? I can't think what to tell you. There's nothing left. Is that when the story ends?

Memory lies on a picnic blanket by the river. Memory's eyes are closed but Memory isn't sleeping. Memory can't sleep anymore, even when Memory wants to. Cotton floats down from the sky in unmade sweaters, landing softly in the river. Memory's friends are nearby. Echo and Moment recite Robert Hass, passing around a bottle of rosé. Memory thought it was too sweet, but Memory took a big swig anyway. Memory's worried that soon their voices will be carried off with the cotton. Memory will jump in and go after them. Memory promises. Memory isn't always honest. Memory wants to swim and swim and swim. Memory wants to drown in their voices, but Memory can't hear them anymore. Memory wants to lie here with eyes closed forever, rather than open them and see that they've gone. On and on. Memory practices words until ache replaces angst. *Swift. Swept. Castoff. Runoff. Riverbed. Deliver. Bed.*

Was coming home a kind of death?

Los Angeles is a desert.
You can drive a car down its river.

Nothing floats. Nothing's carried.

Yesterday, I learned that when you die, there are places beyond fire your body can go where scientists can study the way you decompose in water. They'll put you in a river even as you cross it. But they can't know what whispers enter the marsh of our ears. What is fed to us as we disappear.

I was obsessed with the water,

how it had mastered the art of leaving.
But I lost only my sunglasses in the crossing,

unprecious to me except for possession.

There was a small sliver of island at the center where we swam, swaddled by a roar easily mistaken for rage. Swaths of moss lipped lusciously in the undertow, long and silky like M's hair, thick, slick waves petting flushed hands. To get there you had to risk losing. L and I were always willing. The day he lost his shoes, there was a contrail between the trees on each shore like a tightrope for the gods. Am I remembering wrong? He recovered the shoes. The years hide the truth like fish in muddy water.

Memory looks out the window. The clouds are spelling rain. Memory mimics the glass panes. Says, *Rivulets.* Says, *Leak.* Says, *Burst.* Says, *Weep.*

A year in the desert. D's voice was a stranger's over the phone after so long trying to forget him. A coyote loped past me on the trail when he confessed, friendly as a dog. How dramatic. Then again, *betrayal* is inherently a dramatic word. It's true, a person can become addicted to another person. The night before, I coupled with a man I did not love. On the drive back, I peed on the side of the road. On the other side, a turkey vulture stood over the body of a raccoon but did not bend to eat. The night was hot and thick with moisture that wouldn't fall. We're all capable of inconsistency. Betrayal? I feared my stomach would churn after the first red meat I ate in years, would reject the foreign blood, the salt and fat of a body not my own. I waited shamefully all night for a consequence that did not come.

Still, we talked of returning. To the river, if not the boat. There, all wrongs could be made right. We believed that. Enough to gather like rainwater in the belly of a leaf. Water like a muscle. Water like a tongue. How insistent I was about steering. About paddling. The branches that pierced us. Our breathing, incredulous puffs of half-laughter, that soothed us.

Who says every ending is a beginning?

End here. Begin there.
Again. Here. Again. There.

We are everything that happens in-between.

Memory sleeps in today. Memory has nothing to do but read. Later, Memory will have pancakes with blueberries and butter and a flood of syrup. Memory will do a lot of sighing. Memory will think of calling but won't. Memory will write a letter, but the prospect of buying stamps will be too great, so Memory will give up and drop the letter in a drawer like a sinking stone. Memory will fish it out many months later and read the words Memory wrote. *Well. Miss. Walks. Sad. Spring. Rhododendron. Float. Trip. Lemonade. You.*

Only L picks up the phone nowadays. When he answers, I say,
Have you heard anything?
No, he says, *have you heard anything?*
No, I say.

When things were still new and already destined to die, we went camping near the water to see Comet Neowise, the cold torch of it. Its fire, as with everything, only a gift of the sun, only rock and ice and gas, convinced of its endurance…

And yet we went to experience its fleetingness, to celebrate it, offering ourselves to the blazing mouths of mosquitoes, their familiar abuse, for a blip in the dark, for a river of dust. I burned myself in the waiting for it, endured even when my womanhood set fire to itself—surge of red flame, blue cat scratch in the night, white marble, rolling.

When at last it erupted into our vision, I turned away, watched the coals of our earthly fire die instead. No one went to stoke it, the others huddled together, their necks craned backwards, that unobtainable warmth in their eyes. And when a single ember at the center was all that remained, I cupped my hands full at the lapping edge, freezing from snowmelt, and let it twinkle down to douse the light. The sadness—I refused to explain it. Only the stars witnessed my outpouring, twin comets that descended the sky of my face.

How much will we allow to pass us by?

I want to know where we're headed,
what insurmountable distances trail us.

I want to still be looking ahead, even upon arrival.

Memory collects all kinds of things when Memory dreams, the way foam collects through the battering of waves. In this wave of sleep, the smell of a dirt road after rain. The sharp plastic fumes of cheap inflatable rafts. Childhood likes and dislikes. Growth. The hold of a hand, the sweet texture of pages in a favorite book, the both of them colliding, that hand with the soft feel of paper. The body. Scar of sharp river rock. Sting of cold water. Harsh caw of rooftop crow. Delicate warble of the Dark-eyed Junco. Campfire smoke. Uneven ring of charred stones.

Memory collects moments and echoes of moments. Most of all, Memory collects words. When Memory wakes at midnight in a room walled with windows, the inescapable dark roiling like whitewater beyond, Memory wades through all the words Memory's collected, bobbing like buoys in the drowning night. Some words Memory returns to multiple times. *Ripple. Babble. Trickle. Rush. Crush. Hush. Grieve. Sieve. Grieve. Love. Brief. Love. Grief. Love...*

This morning, in the city I chose, I thought *fog*, and then, no, *smog*, looking out over the dry hills, the sound of the freeway drifting up, having never ceased. Give it the right circumstances. Given the right circumstances, a smile can be unexplainable. Explained away. A ways away, a woman who was not me—who was only a memory of me—stopped beneath a eucalyptus tree to pull a blood orange from her pocket. Humming, she peeled it in the dappled shade, the shadow-branches tattooing her skin. Juice rivered the land of her hands down to her elbows, skin gleaming in the wake, and the first drop that divorced from the body to interrogate the indefinite air plummeted unquestionably to the earth, its brief, undramatic course ending. Ended.

Shall I begin here?

Ariel Machell is a poet from California. She received her BA in English from the University of Southern California, where she was the recipient of the 2018 University of Edinburgh Fellowship, and the Gene and Etta Silverman Family Award. She later received an MFA in Poetry from the University of Oregon in 2021. Her work has been nominated for Best New Poets, and has been published in *Brink, Birdcoat Quarterly, The McNeese Review, The Pinch, SWWIM, The Shore, Up the Staircase Quarterly* and elsewhere. She currently resides in Los Angeles.